Safari Animals™

JACKALS

Maddie Gibbs

PowerKiDS press

New York

Published in 2011 by The Rosen Publishing Group, Inc.
29 East 21st Street, New York, NY 10010

First Edition

Editor: Amelie von Zumbusch
Layout Design: Greg Tucker

Photo Credits: Cover, pp. 5, 6–7, 9, 11, 13, 15, 17, 20–21, 23, 24 (top right), 24 (bottom left), 24 (bottom right) Shutterstock.com; pp. 19, 24 (top left) Richard Packwood/Getty Images.

Library of Congress Cataloging-in-Publication Data

Gibbs, Maddie.
 Jackals / Maddie Gibbs. — 1st ed.
     p. cm. — (Safari animals)
 Includes index.
 ISBN 978-1-4488-2505-9 (library binding) — ISBN 978-1-4488-2596-7 (pbk.) —
 ISBN 978-1-4488-2597-4 (6-pack)
 1. Jackals—Juvenile literature. I. Title.
 QL737.C22G524 2011
 599.77'2—dc22

                                2010018614

Manufactured in the United States of America

CPSIA Compliance Information: Batch #WW11PK: For Further Information contact Rosen Publishing, New York, New York at 1-800-237-9932

CONTENTS

This is a jackal. Jackals are members of the dog family.

Many jackals, such as this **pair**, live in Africa's grasslands and woodlands.

7

Jackals have good eyesight and good hearing. They are smart, too.

9

Jackals most often live in small family groups.

The members of jackal families are close. They often **groom** one another.

13

Jackals call to each other.
They yell, yap, and **howl**.
Jackals can be very loud!

Baby jackals are known as pups. Jackal pups like to play.

Jackal families find **dens** in which their pups can hide. This keeps the pups safe.

19

Jackals hunt for food.
They also eat the
remains of animals
they find.

Jackals eat many kinds of small animals. They eat fruit, too. They drink water.

Words to Know

den

groom

howl

pair

Index

Web Sites

Due to the changing nature of Internet links, PowerKids Press has developed an online list of Web sites related to the subject of this book. This site is updated regularly. Please use this link to access the list: www.powerkidslinks.com/safari/jackals/